CHARLOTTE BOO

THE HYKSOS ꞮOD IN EGYP꞉

SHIRE EGYPTOLOGY

2

Cover illustrations
(Clockwise from top left)
The Hyksos leader Absha portrayed in the tomb of Khnum-hotep II (photograph: Ulla Kaer Andersen). Tell el-Yahudiyeh ware – diagonal punctured-lines design (copyright: Petrie Museum of Egyptian Archaeology, University College London, UC 13465). The Speos Artemidos temple of Hatshepsut (photograph: Wayne Frostick)

British Library Cataloguing in Publication Data:
Booth, Charlotte
The Hyksos Period in Egypt. – (Shire Egyptology; 27)
1. Hyksos 2. Egypt – History – To 332 B.C.
3. Egypt – Antiquities
I. Title 932'.013
ISBN-10: 0 7478 0638 1
ISBN-13: 978 0 7478 0638 1

Published in 2005 by
SHIRE PUBLICATIONS LTD
Cromwell House, Church Street, Princes Risborough,
Buckinghamshire HP27 9AA, UK.

Series Editor: Angela P. Thomas

Number 27 in the Shire Egyptology series.

ISBN-10: 0 7478 0638 1.
ISBN-13: 978 0 7478 0638 1.

First published 2005.

Printed in Malta by Gutenberg Press Ltd, Gudja Road, Tarxien PLA19, Malta.

Contents

Acknowledgements

I would like to thank John Tait and David Jeffreys from the Institute of Archaeology, and the staff at the Petrie Museum, University College London, for all of their help. I want especially to thank Wayne Frostick, who proof-read the manuscript and offered many valuable suggestions, as well as providing many of the photographs. The illustrations are acknowledged as follows: Ulla Kaer Andersen (8, 9, 10 and 11); Wayne Frostick (2, 3, 21, 22, 31 and 32); the Petrie Museum of Egyptian Archaeology, University College London (13, 25, 26, 27 and 28); The Trustees of The British Museum, London (12 and 29); Andrew Walpole (23 and 24); Geoff Webb (33). All other photographs and drawings are by the author.

4

List of illustrations

1. Table of excavations at Tell el Dab'a *page 6*
2. Speos Artemidos temple of Hatshepsut *page 10*
3. Speos Artemidos inscription *page 11*
4. Obelisk-shaped stela showing a soldier with an Asiatic beard *page 13*
5. Deputy Chief Steward Imeny, son of an Asiatic woman *page 13*
6. Thirteenth Dynasty palace: plan *page 14*
7. Head from a statue of an Asiatic noble *page 15*
8. Tomb of Khnum-hotep II, Beni Hasan *page 16*
9. Tomb of Khnum-hotep II, detail of Absha *page 16*
10. Tomb of Khnum-hotep II, detail showing armed Asiatics *page 17*
11. Tomb of Khnum-hotep II, detail showing Asiatic women *page 17*
12. Ivory sphinx of Khayan *page 18*
13. Head of an Asiatic male *page 19*
14. Profile of the head of the Asiatic male *page 19*
15. Hyksos camp at Tell el-Yahudiyeh *page 21*
16. Middle Kingdom houses, Egyptian and Syrian *page 23*
17. Sacred precinct of Tell el Dab'a *page 26*
18. Seth, the primary god of the Hyksos at Tell el Dab'a *page 29*
19. Seth Ba'al from the 400 Year Stela *page 30*
20. Tomb designs of the Hyksos Period *page 32*
21. Stela of Amenhotep III practising archery from a chariot *page 36*
22. Composite and self-bows *page 37*
23. Reconstructions of Levantine weapons *page 38*
24. Asiatic weapons *page 38*
25. Tell el-Yahudiyeh ware – white-painted juglet *page 41*
26. Tell el-Yahudiyeh ware – white-painted juglet *page 41*
27. Tell el-Yahudiyeh ware – vertical bands of herringbone design *page 42*
28. Tell el-Yahudiyeh ware – diagonal punctured-lines design *page 42*
29. Sphinx of Khayan from Baghdad *page 43*
30. Door jamb of Sakir-Har *page 44*
31. Sphinx of Apophis *page 45*
32. Kamose stela *page 47*
33. Mummy of Ahmose *page 49*
34. Map of Egypt and the Near East *page 50*
35. Map of Tell el Dab'a *page 51*

Chronology

(After W. J. Murnane, *The Penguin Guide to Ancient Egypt*, 1983.)

Predynastic	5000–3050 BC
Early Dynastic	3050–2686 BC
Old Kingdom	2686–2181 BC
First Intermediate Period	2181–2040 BC
Middle Kingdom	2040–1782 BC
Second Intermediate Period	1782–1570 BC
Thirteenth Dynasty	1782–1650 BC

     Wegaf
     Ameny Intef IV
     Hor
     Sobekhotep II (Amenemhat VI)
     Khendjer
     Sobekhotep III
     Neferhotep I
     Sobekhotep IV
     Ay
     Neferhotep II

Fourteenth Dynasty
     Nehesy

Fifteenth Dynasty	1663–1570 BC

     Shamuqenu
     'Aper-'Anati
     Sakir-Har
     Khayan Sewoserenre
     Apophis Awoserre/Aqenenre/Nebkhepeshre
     Khamudy Hotepibre

Sixteenth Dynasty	1663–1540 BC

     Anather
     Yakobaam

Seventeenth Dynasty	1663–1570 BC

     Sekhemre Shedtawy Sobekemsaf II
     Nubkheperre Intef VII
     Sanakhtenre Tao I
     Seqenenre Tao II
     Kamose

New Kingdom	1570–1070 BC
Ahmose I	1570–1546 BC
Amenhotep I	1551–1524 BC
Tuthmosis I	1524–1518 BC
Tuthmosis II	1518–1504 BC
Tuthmosis III	1504–1450 BC
Hatshepsut	1498–1483 BC
Amenhotep II	1453–1419 BC
Third Intermediate Period	1070–664 BC
Late Period	525–332 BC
Ptolemaic Period	332–30 BC

1
Introduction

The Hyksos Period in Egypt has intrigued Egyptologists for many years,
but because of fragmentary archaeological and textual resources it has
been much neglected in favour of the other, archaeologically richer,
periods of Egyptian history.

The fall of the Middle Kingdom in 1782 BC heralded the start of the
Second Intermediate Period, which was characterised by the division of
Egypt into different regions, each ruled by a petty chieftain. This period
is made up of five dynasties, ruling mostly contemporaneously with
each other. The early Thirteenth Dynasty (c.1782–1720 BC) ruled all of
Egypt until King Sobekhotep or King Meneferure (the twenty-fourth and
twenty-seventh rulers). There is little evidence of the rulers after these
kings north of the Abydos region, indicating that the north of Egypt and the
Delta were independently ruled at this time. The latter part of the Thirteenth
Dynasty ruled both the north and the south of Egypt.

The Fourteenth Dynasty consisted of many kings ruling simultaneously
in different areas of the north of Egypt and the Delta. Some of these
rulers may have been vassal kings of the Thirteenth or the Fifteenth
Dynasty. In the *Turin Canon* (a papyrus dated to the reign of Ramses II,
which lists about three hundred rulers of Egypt) the Fourteenth Dynasty
is attributed with more than fifty kings, indicating a particularly unstable
dynasty characterised by short reigns. At this time there would have

DATE	DYNASTY	MATERIAL CULTURE / POPULATION
Before 1750 BC	12th	Middle Bronze Age IIA plus Egyptian Middle Kingdom
1750-1680 BC	13th	Middle Bronze Age IIA plus Egyptian Middle Kingdom
1680-1660 BC	14th	Middle Bronze Age IIA - Middle Bronze Age IIB transitional
1660-1610 BC	15th	Middle Bronze Age IIB – Early Hyksos
1610-1590 BC	15th	Middle Bronze Age IIB - Hyksos
1590-1570 BC	15th	Middle Hyksos Period
1570-1540 BC	15th	Middle Bronze Age IIC Late Hyksos Period
1540 BC	18th	Late Bronze Age – site abandoned

1. Table of excavations at Tell el Dab'a.

been a number of fortresses on the borders of the eastern Delta, to guard against the Canaanites, and possibly along the western borders, to guard against the Libyans. It has been suggested that from these fortresses the numerous kings of the Fourteenth Dynasty rose to power.

The Fifteenth Dynasty (1663–1570 BC) is normally attributed to the Hyksos kings, known in ancient Egyptian as the *hk3 h3swt* or 'rulers of foreign lands'. They initially ruled the eastern Delta from their capital at Avaris (modern Tell el Dab'a), although later in their reign they gradually extended their power over middle and southern Egypt. The kings of the Fifteenth Dynasty are the only rulers of this period known by the title *hk3 h3swt*, although the Middle Kingdom tomb of Khnum-hotep II at Beni Hasan shows the leader of an Asiatic trading party referred to thus. Shortly after the start of the Fifteenth Dynasty (1663 BC) the Thirteenth Dynasty (1782–1650 BC) ended and the Seventeenth Dynasty (1663–1570 BC) began in the Theban area, indicating an era of change. The Sixteenth Dynasty was also current in the western Delta at this time, although the Hyksos Fifteenth Dynasty probably did not consider it to be a threat to its own growing power, perhaps because its leaders were vassal kings.

Nubia, south of the Egyptian border, had also managed to pull away from the power of a weakening Egypt and declared its own kings in the Egyptian style. These numerous contemporaneous dynasties throughout Egypt indicate the state of upheaval the country was in during the Second Intermediate Period, with Egypt divided up into many pieces. From these dynasties rose two strong leaders, whose main ambition was to unite Egypt and rule as King of Upper and Lower Egypt. These two powers were the Fifteenth Dynasty Hyksos kings, ruling from Avaris in the Delta, and the Theban Seventeenth Dynasty. During their ninety-year reign the Hyksos kings campaigned southwards until they had gained power over the Theban region, albeit for a relatively short period, and then the Theban Seventeenth Dynasty started to push them northwards in an attempt to reconquer the land taken.

One of the most debated issues surrounding the Hyksos rulers of the Fifteenth Dynasty is their ethnic origin, as it is widely accepted that they were not Egyptian but had Asiatic roots. It is generally agreed that they came from Palestine because the material culture of Avaris is very closely correlated to the last stage of the Middle Bronze Age II from the Syro-Palestinian region. Despite this general concurrence there is evidence to suggest that there were also Mesopotamian influences within the Hyksos culture. There is a record of a female slave called Ishtar-ummi being captured by an Egyptian during the wars near the end of the Hyksos reign. Her name belongs to a Northern Mesopotamian culture and not the Canaanite culture, in which it would have been 'Astarteummi'. However, using names to trace origins is not always accurate as names sometimes travel more widely than physical cultures.

In the Amada stela of Amenhotep II the Hyksos are listed alongside the Retenu, a general term used for the Palestinians, suggesting that the Egyptians regarded them as a different ethnic group from the Palestinians. There are also many Mesopotamian influences in the material culture of the Hyksos – composite bows, scimitars, chariots, cylinder seal designs, vaulted burials and toggle pins. All of these objects originate from Mesopotamia as far back as 750 years before their arrival in Egypt during the Hyksos rule. Although this may suggest that the Hyksos came from the Mesopotamian region it seems unusual that when introduced to Egypt these objects were of the older, traditional Mesopotamian styles rather than the modern examples being used in Mesopotamia at the time. It is possible that the objects did not reach the Hyksos directly from Mesopotamia but through connections with other nations. There is not enough conclusive evidence that the Hyksos originated in Mesopotamia; it seems more probable that they were Canaanite with Mesopotamian influences.

2
The rise of the Hyksos

'Unexpectedly from the regions of the east, invaders of obscure race marched in confidence in victory against our land. By main force they easily seized it without striking a blow.' This is how Manetho (c.300 BC) reported the start of the Hyksos Period. Although his accounts are generally not considered accurate there is very little archaeological evidence to suggest a violent take-over of the throne at this time.

At the Middle Kingdom's collapse, thought to be the result of many years of famine and disease, Egypt was in a state of political and economic upheaval. During any period of natural disaster the king was held responsible. He was seen as an intermediary between the gods and mortals and it was therefore his duty to appease the gods on behalf of the people; should his relationship with the gods break down then this would result in disaster for Egypt. This would lead to political unrest and a desire to replace the king with one who would please the gods and re-establish the cosmic order of Maat.

Although thought to relate to the collapse of central government during the First Intermediate Period, the *Admonitions of Ipuwer* is also considered applicable to the start of the Second Intermediate Period. The *Admonitions* state that the elite positions in society at this time were in jeopardy because of the uprisings of the poor: 'The wealthy are in mourning. The poor man is full of joy. Every town says: let us suppress the powerful among us.' However, despite this description evidence suggests that after the Hyksos gained power they kept the existing Egyptian administration system and used established Egyptian officials as a tool to gain support from the resident Egyptian community.

Egypt's fragile political state at the end of the Middle Kingdom could have laid the country open to invasion from a number of foreign groups, from both external and internal positions. The Hyksos, however, took advantage of the situation and overthrew the petty kings who were at the time claiming sovereignty in different areas of the Delta. The Hyksos' strength and ability to take over seemingly effortlessly can be attributed to a number of factors.

From the existing archaeological evidence it is apparent that the Hyksos were a warrior people. At Tell el Dab'a a number of weapons were discovered as burial goods. Eighty per cent of these weapons were of Syro-Palestinian origin (duck-bill axe, socketed axe, lance head) and were found to be present in fifty per cent of male burials. In the Twelfth Dynasty many Asiatics would have been recruited into the Egyptian army for their battle skills. It is widely believed that the Hyksos introduced the horse and chariot to Egypt, and this has been used to explain how they took over the throne so easily. However, both the Hyksos and the Egyptians learned the battle skills of horse and chariot together at the end of the Fifteenth Dynasty.

Although they were a nation of warriors, there seems to be little evidence that the Hyksos staged a violent take-over. The variations between the pottery of the Fourteenth and Fifteenth Dynasties are subtle and suggest a peaceful change-over in political leadership, and any style change can be attributed to the personal ambitions of a new king. Avaris, although being a fortified city, does not seem to have been engaged in battle; indeed the reinforced enclosure wall was not built until the very end of the period (1603–1570 BC), when there would have been problems with the Seventeenth Dynasty Theban kings. However, once the Hyksos Fifteenth Dynasty had seized power from the petty chieftains it took their army twenty years to travel southwards from Avaris to Abydos and a further thirty years to gain control over the Theban area. This extended length of time may suggest that there was resistance from petty chieftains trying to retain power.

If the Egyptian literary evidence is to be believed, the Hyksos caused mass destruction throughout Egypt on this march south. However, these

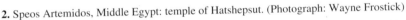

2. Speos Artemidos, Middle Egypt: temple of Hatshepsut. (Photograph: Wayne Frostick)

3. The inscription regarding the Hyksos, on the exterior of the Speos Artemidos. (Photograph: Wayne Frostick)

sources were written after the expulsion of the Hyksos with the purpose of reinforcing ideologies of Egyptian kingship. Hatshepsut, in the Speos Artemidos inscription, refers to the Hyksos as 'barbarians' and states that they marched whilst 'overthrowing that which was made'. She casts further aspersions on the Hyksos by claiming that 'they ruled in ignorance of Re'. Hatshepsut reports that during her reign she restored the ruins, and 'raised up that which was unfinished since the Asiatics were in the midst of Avaris' – indicating that the previous rulers, following the Hyksos expulsion, did not attend to this task. This is inaccurate since the restoration of monuments was undertaken by the Theban Seventeenth Dynasty, which was contemporary with the Hyksos Fifteenth Dynasty and a century before the reign of Hatshepsut. During the troubled period before the collapse of the Middle Kingdom the temples may have fallen into disuse and disrepair because the more pressing issues of famine led to their neglect. Any building works started before the collapse would not have been continued if the country was suffering from disaster. Once the Hyksos were in power their priorities would have been the building of their new capital at Avaris; the old projects were soon forgotten.

The *Unwetterstela*, written in the reign of Ahmose I (1570–1546 BC), first king of the Eighteenth Dynasty, also refers to the mass destruction of temples and monuments by the Hyksos rulers. The damage is caused by a storm, a metaphor for the foreign rulers. However, the phraseology used suggests that some monuments fell into disrepair naturally: 'His majesty then ordered the repair of the chapels which had fallen in ruins in all the country.' The text also refers to the sacred chambers of the temples being invaded by the water and the subsequent need to restore them since they have been de-sanctified. The *Unwetterstela* is referring to the metaphorical sense of invasion: the feeling of violation induced by foreigners being allowed into the places reserved solely for Egyptian rulers. Rebuilding and restoring were ways of eradicating the existence of the Hyksos invasion, as well as legitimising the rule of the new king.

There is evidence of Hyksos destruction and usurpation of statues but nothing on the scale recorded in the Speos Artemidos inscription or the *Unwetterstela*. This destruction and usurpation took place only under the later reigns of Apophis and Khayan and is a traditional Egyptian practice – every king usurped statues of earlier kings to adorn their temples and capitals. The worst damage was carried out at the temple of Ptah at Memphis, which was looted during the reign of Apophis. Apophis also usurped the Middle Kingdom monumental sphinxes of Amenemhat III found at Tanis, although he would originally have set them up at Avaris, as well as a Twelfth Dynasty offering stand, on which he inscribed his name alongside that of his wife, Princess Tany, possibly a Theban princess (her name is Theban). Khayan usurped an earlier king's Ka statue from Bubastis and set it up in his own Ka temple at Avaris. A number of Thirteenth Dynasty monuments were also taken to Avaris in order to give the city a royal appearance. These monuments were later retrieved from Avaris by Ramesses II and taken to Pi-Ramesses; they were then taken to Tanis by the Twenty-first and Twenty-second Dynasties. There were also a number of Middle Kingdom statues in the Levant, Aegean and Sudan that could have represented diplomatic gifts from the Hyksos rulers. The early kings of the Fifteenth Dynasty, with their small-scale local ambition, do not appear to have usurped earlier royal monuments, indicating that the later kings, encouraged by their own ambition and rising power, had more monumental works at the Hyksos capital and, in the Egyptian fashion, usurped the earlier kings' examples. Although this was common practice for the Egyptians, however, it aroused anger in them when carried out by foreigners.

The *Admonitions of Ipuwer* give a clear picture of the upheaval faced by the citizens of Egypt during either the First or the Second Intermediate Period. As well as harbouring a general feeling of distrust – 'a man looks upon his son as his enemy' – the people were facing real danger

4. Obelisk-shaped stela showing a soldier with an Asiatic beard. (Drawing by Charlotte Booth after Bietak, 1996)

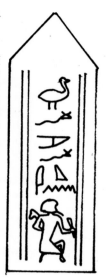

from 'the tribes of the deserts' moving into the Nile Valley. 'The wrongdoer is everywhere ... the plunderer is everywhere'; consequently 'the robber is a possessor of riches, the rich man has become a plunderer'. The average citizen would therefore be looking for an escape from these circumstances, either by leaving Egypt or by supporting a new line of kings who would re-establish law and order.

The Hyksos started their rule in the Delta region, where the citizens probably felt a little distanced from the religious capital at Thebes. By offering their support, the people would have been safeguarding their own and their families' futures. This desperate acceptance would have increased the speed of the Hyksos' ascension to power. The Hyksos community was well established in the Delta region by the end of the Middle Kingdom and would have had local support. The earliest evidence of an Asiatic settlement at Avaris is from the Twelfth Dynasty (1750 BC). Houses from this period were similar to northern Syrian houses, indicating that the community may have originated in that region. They also showed evidence of un-Egyptian burial practices, with the cemeteries in close proximity to the houses. Funerary evidence suggests that a large number of this Middle Kingdom population worked for the Egyptian army. One Avaris resident, the Deputy Chief Steward Imeny, was proud of his Asiatic heritage and even showed himself with an Asiatic beard, although his Egyptian name suggests an integration into Egyptian society. This indicates that Asiatics from the Delta area were able to work their way into positions of power. Further evidence of the adoption of Egyptian lifestyle by the Asiatic Delta community is found in the Thirteenth Dynasty 'palace' at Avaris, which is purely Egyptian in style and could be an extended elite Middle Kingdom Egyptian house. This

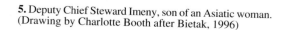

5. Deputy Chief Steward Imeny, son of an Asiatic woman. (Drawing by Charlotte Booth after Bietak, 1996)

6. Thirteenth Dynasty palace. (Drawing by Charlotte Booth after Bietak, 1996)

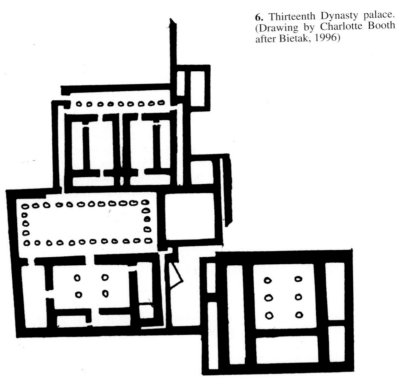

palace had a large court with pillars, aligned on all sides with a central pool or tank. An extension was built on to the palace but was never completed. The palace also contained a garden of trees in neat lines and flower-beds set into grids. In a later period two tombs were dug into the garden and probably belonged to officials of the palace. They appear to be Asiatics, although the tombs were Egyptian in style with a tree pit in front of the entrance. This palace is thought to have belonged to the ninth ruler of the Thirteenth Dynasty, Sehetepibre Hornetdjhertyef, 'the Asiatics' son', believed to be an Asiatic petty chieftain, who perhaps was one of the earliest *hk3 h3swt*, although it is likely that he was subordinate to Egyptian officials. The palace seems to have been abandoned – perhaps the result of the resident official's disgrace.

An Asiatic settlement was then built on top of this palace area but was abruptly abandoned and replaced with numerous mass graves, indicating that there may have been an epidemic in the region. Whole families were buried simultaneously and studies of the remains show the health of the population here in all periods to have been very poor. There was no conclusive sign of an epidemic but general poor health leads to easier infection. The *Hearst* and the *London Medical Papyrus* refer to the 'Asiatic sickness' in the early Eighteenth Dynasty, which may have been the bubonic plague. Study of the human remains also shows that the bodies were Levantine and not Egyptian in origin.

In the period just before the Hyksos dynasty (1750–1680 BC) there was an influx of Canaanites into the Delta area. A twenty to forty per cent increase in Syro-Palestinian pottery found at Avaris indicates a rise in the Asiatic population there. This influx would have occurred just before the years of famine that led to the Middle Kingdom's collapse, and so was not a conscious effort on the Asiatics' part to invade Egypt. By 1663 BC, when the Hyksos Fifteenth Dynasty began, they had already been living in the eastern Delta for one hundred years and would have been fourth-generation Egyptians. It would have been an effortless transition into power for them, as they would already have been a major part of the community.

It has been suggested that rather than taking over from within the Delta region the Hyksos were chieftains from Canaan who took over Avaris first, because of the resident Canaanite population. However, the lack of contemporary evidence in Canaan of the Fifteenth Dynasty does not confirm this theory. If the Hyksos were invaders from Canaan there would have been increased trade with this area, but this is not supported by the archaeological record. Trade with Canaan did continue but with diminished frequency after the start of the Hyksos Period. Fewer Fifteenth Dynasty seals were found in the Canaan area than Fourteenth Dynasty ones – although this could be explained by the lower quantities manufactured, as the Fifteenth Dynasty seals were used only by the king whereas those from the Fourteenth Dynasty were also used by officials.

There is limited evidence of the appearance of the Hyksos, but from the evidence available it is clear that they were Asiatic in origin. A statue of a Hyksos dignitary was found at Tell el Dab'a that shows very un-Egyptian characteristics, with the figure wearing a mushroom-style wig and clutching a throw stick on his right shoulder. The tomb of

7. Head from a statue of an Asiatic noble (from Tell el Dab'a). (Drawing by Charlotte Booth after Bietak, 1996)

8. (Above) Tomb of Khnum-hotep II, Beni Hasan. (Photograph: Ulla Kaer Andersen)

9. Tomb of Khnum-hotep II: detail of Absha, the leader of the *hk3 h3swt*. (Photograph: Ulla Kaer Andersen)

10. Tomb of Khnum-hotep II: detail of the Hyksos, showing armed Asiatics. (Photograph: Ulla Kaer Andersen)

11. Tomb of Khnum-hotep II: detail of the Hyksos, showing Asiatic women. (Photograph: Ulla Kaer Andersen)

Khnum-hotep II at Beni Hasan has an image of the leader of the trading party, Absha, with the title *hk3 h3swt* above his head. His Asiatic dress and beard identify his origins. An ivory sphinx, found in an Abydos tomb, shows what appears to be an Egyptian king with Asiatic features holding a struggling Egyptian between his paws. The face was originally thought to represent Khayan, although this has been disputed and it is now thought to represent a Middle Kingdom king. However, the profile shows a hooked nose very similar to that of Absha and looks more Asiatic than Egyptian, whereas the figure between his feet does look more Egyptian. The whole image seems to be a role reversal.

The Fifteenth Dynasty consists of six primary kings, although the exact reign length for the earlier kings is uncertain.

1. Shamuqenu – 1663 BC–?
2. 'Aper-'Anati – ?
3. Sakir-Har ?–1649 BC
4. Khayan Sewoserenre – 1649–1609 BC
5. Apophis Awoserre/Aqenenre/Nebkhepeshre – 1609–1569 BC
6. Khamudy Hotepibre – 1569–1570 BC

Many other kings are mentioned on scarabs, indicating a possible internal struggle or the distribution of scarabs to those who were not kings. Scarabs may have been issued to crown princes or may record earlier names of the six primary kings (Apophis changed his prenomen at least twice). The most problematic king of this type was King Nehesy, who is recorded as having an heir, a prenomen, a long reign and numerous monuments – suggesting that he was a king in his own right. His worship of Seth points to a position in the Fifteenth Dynasty, although he is not one of the traditional six. He has the title 'King's eldest son' and is believed to be Khayan's or Apophis' eldest son, although he may have only used the title to legitimise his reign. His origins are obscure; it has been suggested that his father was actually an Egyptian official rather than a Hyksos king. Nehesy, however, was a king of the Fourteenth Dynasty ruling the south Delta. Many of his monuments have been found at Avaris, indicating that he would have had some connections with the Hyksos capital. The name 'Nehesy' resembles the Egyptian word for 'the Nubian', although his northern

12. The ivory sphinx of Khayan. (Photograph: copyright The Trustees of The British Museum, London, BM EA 679)

13. Head of an Asiatic male. (Copyright: Petrie Museum of Egyptian Archaeology, University College London, UC 33278)

domain points more to an Asiatic origin for this king.

The first four rulers of the Fifteenth Dynasty (Shamuqenu, 'Aper-'Anati, Sakir-Har and Khayan) used the *hk3 h3swt* title, although it was abandoned by Khayan when he gained control over Upper and Lower Egypt. It could be suggested that the Hyksos rulers did not have the ambition originally to call themselves by typical Egyptian royal titles and seemed content with ruling the Delta under this title. At the beginning of their reign the country was divided into three with the Hyksos Fifteenth Dynasty (1663–1570 BC) ruling in the Delta, the Fourteenth and the Sixteenth Dynasties (1663–1540 BC) ruling in the western Delta and the Seventeenth Dynasty (1663–1570 BC) in the Theban region. The

14. Profile of the Asiatic head shown in figure 13. (Drawing by Charlotte Booth)

Hyksos waited twenty years at Memphis gaining strength and support before campaigning southwards to conquer Abydos. The lack of evidence for the first three kings of the Hyksos Fifteenth Dynasty could coincide with this small-scale local ambition. The ambition of these kings gradually increased and the boundaries of Hyksos rule were fully defined in the reign of Apophis, the strongest of the Hyksos kings. The southern boundary was at Hermopolis and the northern boundary is defined in the Nitokris Adoption Stela as being at Pi-Hathor between Tanis and Bubastis. However, there is evidence of isolated Hyksos points of control at Nefrusi (in Middle Egypt) and Gebelein (south of Luxor), which would have secured a safe trading passage from Avaris to Nubia. This suggests that the Theban Seventeenth Dynasty may have been a vassal of the Hyksos kings.

3
Settlements

The capital city of the Hyksos was Avaris (modern-day Tell el Dab'a) in the eastern Delta. The site has been extensively excavated and is rich in Hyksos Period architecture and burials, and is the only site that can be dated accurately to this period. Other sites in Egypt have, however, produced architecture thought to be contemporary with the Hyksos Period.

The site of Tell el-Yahudiyeh was identified as a Hyksos settlement by Petrie. He identified Palestinian pottery known as Tell el-Yahudiyeh ware, which is also common at Tell el Dab'a. At Tell el-Yahudiyeh, Petrie discovered the mud-brick ruins of a town that he dated to the Fifteenth Dynasty. The settlement was enclosed in an 18 metre sand bank with a 61 metre slope leading to the eastern entrance. This sand bank was surrounded by a three-brick deep and 12 metre high wall; very little remains of the wall as it was removed in the nineteenth

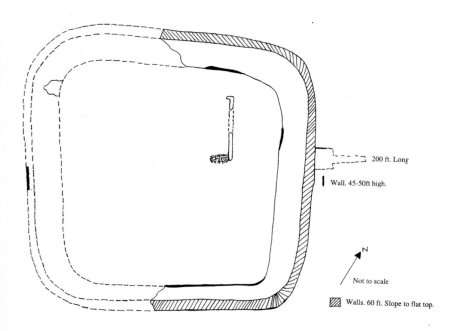

200 ft. Long

Wall. 45-50ft high.

N

Not to scale

Walls. 60 ft. Slope to flat top.

15. The Hyksos camp at Tell el-Yahudiyeh. (Drawing by Charlotte Booth after Petrie, 1906)

century for building material. There were five graves within the enclosure, each containing Hyksos scarabs. One was a gold-mounted scarab inscribed with Khayan's name, which would date this grave to 1621–1581 BC at the earliest.

This type of settlement is very un-Egyptian in design but would have been an ideal defensive system as the high sand banks gave an extensive view of the desert and the long slope exposed anyone approaching from a great distance. There is little doubt that the Hyksos were at this site, as the scarabs suggest, but there has been some debate over the dating of the site. It has been suggested that this settlement was a New Kingdom enclosure as a town dated to the reign of Ramesses III is situated here, cutting across the Hyksos enclosure wall.

Another type of defensive system that may have been used in the Hyksos Period is the loophole system found at the Middle Kingdom fortress of Buhen in Nubia, thought to have been built during the co-regency between Amenemhat I and Senusret I (1971–1928 BC). Although this site is earlier than the Hyksos Period evidence suggests, its architectural style may still have been available during this period. The loopholes allow the archer to fire arrows in three different directions at the enemy below. It is suggested in the Kamose stela that this type of system was used at the time of the Hyksos: 'I beheld his women on the roof of the palace peering through the loopholes.'

The Asiatic settlement in the Delta region dates from 1750–1570 BC and began as an outpost built by First Intermediate Period kings to monitor the Asiatic infiltration into the area, which then developed into the vibrant capital city of the Hyksos kings. Tell el Dab'a was situated on a feeder channel from the Pelusiac branch of the Nile, which created a large, natural lake. A channel draining from this lake made the water levels controllable at the site, which resulted in Tell el Dab'a becoming a major harbour and serving as a base for maritime trading and expeditions. It may have had a seafaring population from the earliest times. On the Old Kingdom temple of Sahure and the causeway of Unas, Asiatics are represented manning the ships that brought in slaves from Syria. There is similar imagery from the New Kingdom, so it is likely that in the Thirteenth Dynasty Asiatics, especially from coastal Levant, were used in Egypt for their maritime skills.

Tell el Dab'a is made up of three mounds, with a natural lake basin just north of the south-western mound. The central mound was occupied by the Twelfth Dynasty settlement, the south-western mound was occupied by settlements of the Twelfth, Thirteenth and Fifteenth Dynasties, and the northern mound was occupied by the New Kingdom settlement. The Hyksos settlement was situated on the south-western mound, which is about 500 metres in diameter.

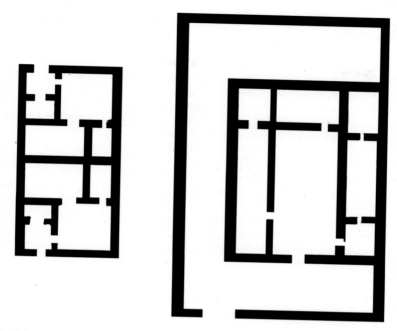

16. Middle Kingdom houses, Egyptian and Syrian. (Drawing by Charlotte Booth after Bietak, 1996)

The Middle Kingdom settlement, which includes a workers' village, was built by Amenemhat I at the beginning of the Twelfth Dynasty and thrived until the reign of Senwosret I. Although Egyptian in nature, the small amount of Middle Bronze Age II pottery represents contact with semi-nomadic Bedouins and could indicate that the early Twelfth Dynasty settlers were from the northern part of the coastal Levant. However, they were highly Egyptianised when they arrived, and it is suggested that they may have come from the Egyptian colony at Byblos. Over the early Twelfth Dynasty remains had been built a settlement of small mud-brick huts and mud-brick silos for food storage. From this early population, evidence has been found of limestone moulds, crucibles and jets of clay, indicating that a copper industry was flourishing in the area at this time.

The earlier Asiatic settlement (1680–1660 BC) shows Canaanite characteristics, with the houses set a distance apart and the cemeteries in close proximity to the houses. As more people moved to the area after the Hyksos began their rule (1660–1610 BC) the houses were built much closer together, with narrower streets between them, because space became an issue. In 1680–1660 BC the population would have been made up mostly of Asiatics, whereas changes in the 1660–1610 BC period show a larger element of the Egyptian community had also moved to the new capital. The cemetery in this later period was separated from the residential area by a roofed street and was closer to the temple complexes; as an Egyptian custom, this is likely to have occurred as a result of the growing Egyptian population.

As more people went to Tell el Dab'a in the period 1610–1590 BC, the newly discovered Egyptian practices were abandoned because of space restrictions. Small houses were now built in the cemeteries and children were buried in the doorways of the larger houses. In 1590–1570 BC there was more overcrowding and therefore more houses were built in the cemeteries, and as overcrowding increased tombs were incorporated into the architecture of the houses. It would appear that near the end of the Hyksos Period (1600–1570 BC) the rulers felt threatened and a thick enclosure wall was built around the city. Shortly after this period the site was abandoned as the Hyksos were expelled from Egypt.

In the early Hyksos Period the lower classes appeared to build their houses around their master's house; there is not as much evidence of this in the later period because of excessive overcrowding as well as damage caused by modern agriculture. In the north-east periphery area of the settlement the houses were very small, with few remains of animal bones, suggesting a low meat content to the residents' diet and therefore indicating poorer classes. In the eastern area there are large houses with stairs leading to upper floors, indicating that the more affluent of the community lived in this area. In the late Hyksos Period some of the houses had rooms that opened on to the street and these could have been rented out or sold as shops and workshops.

All of the tomb styles and methods of interring the bodies at Tell el Dab'a were Canaanite, although they reflect similar beliefs in the afterlife to those held by the Egyptians: although mummification was not practised, numerous grave goods were buried with the bodies. The most remarkable burial customs practised at Tell el Dab'a are the servant and donkey burials (1680–1660 BC). They became popular around the time of the Asiatic influx into Tell el Dab'a at the beginning of the Hyksos reign. The servants were buried at a different orientation from the tomb owners. They lay across the tomb entrance facing the door, almost as if waiting for instruction. Three of these servant burials have been discovered at Tell el Dab'a, and all the servants appear to have been buried at the same time as the tomb owners, suggesting a custom of servant sacrifice. Although not practised in this period by the Egyptians, this custom had been practised in the Predynastic period. It is also known from the Levant and Canaan.

Seventeen donkey burials have been discovered at Tell el Dab'a, generally found in pairs in front of the tomb entrance. This custom had continued for the majority of the site's history (1750–1570 BC), which shows that a large Asiatic community was present here for the duration of the Hyksos reign. It is possible that, like the servants, the donkeys were sacrificed on the death of the tomb owner since they were also all buried at the same time. One of the donkeys even had offerings buried with it. Donkey burials were practised in northern Syria from the third millennium BC and may have entered Egypt via sea trade. Donkeys were closely associated with caravaneering and the owners may have been expedition leaders. In relation to the total number of burials the percentage of servant and donkey burials is small and could represent the burials of the elite or ruling class of this city.

The Hyksos appear to have been a religious people and the excavations at Tell el Dab'a have uncovered five temples contemporary with this period, which show a mixture of Egyptian and Canaanite styles. Conventions followed for all the temples were the entrances being in the north wall and the temples themselves orientated NNW–SSE.

Temple I is Egyptian in style, with three sanctuaries at the rear of the building. This temple was built between 1680 and 1660 BC and remained in use until 1590 BC, when it fell into ruin. It is contemporary with Temple III, which shows very few Egyptian characteristics, being of Canaanite style, constructed of sandy mud-bricks. In the courtyard there was a free-standing altar or fireplace where sacrifices may have been made. Four 1 metre thick hollow walls surrounded the main hall and sanctuary recess areas. The outside walls were mud-brick and had been whitewashed and show traces of azure-blue paint. In the sacred precinct of Temple III, door jambs belonging to King Nehesy were found. These may originally have stood here or they may have been moved at a later date.

An extended entrance hall was added sometime afterwards and included three doors in the north wall. The need for these additional doors could suggest that the temple, or at least part of it, was open to the public. The entrance hall was possibly roofed and had a sand-brick floor. There was also an eastern door, which connected Temple III with Temple V.

To the north of Temple V was an altar with sacrificial pits in front of it. Sacrificing was a purely Canaanite ritual and was clearly practised in these temples. Despite this custom, the temple itself is built in Egyptian style. It has been suggested that as this temple is connected to Temple

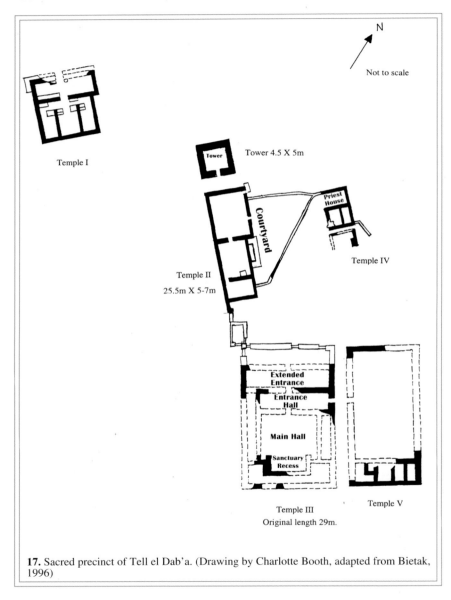

17. Sacred precinct of Tell el Dab'a. (Drawing by Charlotte Booth, adapted from Bietak, 1996)

III by the western door and is in such close proximity to it the two could represent the divine couple Ba'al and Astarte, who may be the deities to whom the temples were dedicated.

Temple II is Canaanite in design, with an offering niche for a statue in the eastern wall with a deposit of a copper harpoon beneath. On the eastern side there is a triangular courtyard, which may also have been used for offerings. To the north of the temple are a tower and a mud-brick tomb chamber. A cemetery from 1680–1660 BC is also in this area, and, although the temple is Canaanite in design, having the cemetery in close proximity to it is an Egyptian custom and suggests a funerary role for this temple. The outside mud-brick walls also have traces of azure-blue paint and some unidentifiable painted figures. There is a three-chambered building to the east of the triangular courtyard, which may be the priests' house, as it is accessible via the courtyard. Just south of this house are the remains of the small Temple IV, which has a stone floor and a niche in the eastern wall.

The design of these temples, being a mixture of Canaanite and Egyptian, reflects the population and religious beliefs of the area. Temples V and I are based on designs of Middle Kingdom houses from Tell el Dab'a.

The city of Avaris would have been very modern in its time and it has been suggested that it may have rivalled Thebes – although the erratic archaeological recovery rate means that this is not obvious. However, excavations have uncovered at Ezbet Hilme (a region of Tell el Dab'a) a 12 metre section of a water channel made of large limestone blocks in a 2.5 metre ditch. The interior faces of the blocks had been smoothed and the outer facings left rough. Most of these limestone blocks had been reused from earlier monuments, and one was even a decorated block from an Old Kingdom mastaba tomb. The whole of the water channel was covered in a thick capping of clay and limestone chips and then the ditch refilled. This water channel would have sloped from north to south and channelled clean Nile water from the Pelusiac branch of the Nile to the buildings in this area. The remains of fish bones found in the channel indicate that the fish were still living whilst in the channel, affirming that the channel and the water remained clean. The channel would have been a local water resource to this section of the city.

On the western edge of Tell el Dab'a is a late Hyksos Period (1600 BC) citadel, one of the buildings that would have benefited from the clean water being channelled in from the Nile. As the land in this area was low-lying, the whole area covered by this palace had been artificially raised in antiquity using dumped materials. A 300 metre enclosure wall surrounded the palace, to the south of which was a two-level garden with trees planted into a grid on the lower level, with potted flowers in long lines. There were also pits that would have been used for shrubs, indicating that there was a vineyard in the area. However, the enclosure wall was probably not just for the protection of the garden. This citadel would have been used by the Egyptian army after the fall of Avaris and the expulsion of the Hyksos. A large amount of Kerma ware discovered here indicates that Nubian archers were resident, and were therefore a legitimate part of the Egyptian army.

4
Religion

The ancient Egyptians are famous for their rich religion and large pantheon of gods, and during the Hyksos Period religion was equally important. There are very limited resources for studying the Hyksos religion, but what is available can give us some clues about their gods and religious practices.

The most important god of the Hyksos was the Egyptian deity Seth, who had been the principal god in the Delta region before their arrival. This is attested by a number of sources. The *Sallier I Papyrus* says 'Apophis took Seth to himself as lord and did not serve any god which was in the entire land except Seth'. There is evidence that King Apophis (1609–1569 BC) worshipped other gods besides Seth, but he did dedicate an altar to 'Seth Lord of Avaris'. The imagery we have of Seth from the

18. Seth, the primary god of the Hyksos at Tell el Dab'a. From Medinet Habu. (Photograph: Charlotte Booth)

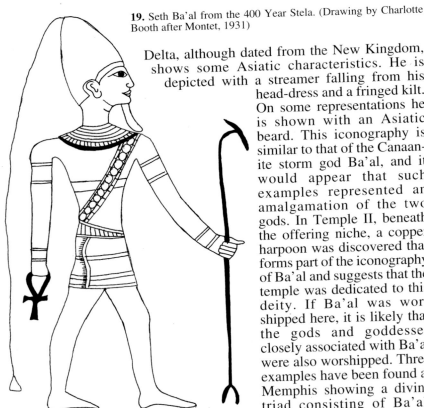

19. Seth Ba'al from the 400 Year Stela. (Drawing by Charlotte Booth after Montet, 1931)

Delta, although dated from the New Kingdom, shows some Asiatic characteristics. He is depicted with a streamer falling from his head-dress and a fringed kilt. On some representations he is shown with an Asiatic beard. This iconography is similar to that of the Canaanite storm god Ba'al, and it would appear that such examples represented an amalgamation of the two gods. In Temple II, beneath the offering niche, a copper harpoon was discovered that forms part of the iconography of Ba'al and suggests that the temple was dedicated to this deity. If Ba'al was worshipped here, it is likely that the gods and goddesses closely associated with Ba'al were also worshipped. Three examples have been found at Memphis showing a divine triad consisting of Ba'al, Reshef (who has very similar characteristics to Ba'al) and the goddess Qudshu, who is shown naked, front facing, holding lilies or serpents in her hands whilst standing on a lion.

Astarte was the goddess of love, war and fertility and Anat was described as the 'milk cow of Seth' and is shown with cow horns, and they were both believed to be the wife or sister of the god Ba'al. On some scarab examples Anat is given the title 'The Mistress of the Two Trees', which implies she could be the Hyksos equivalent of Hathor, Lady of the Sycamore, and votive offerings from this period have been found at Hathor's temple in Gebelein. Near the altar of Temple III at Avaris there are two tree pits that may have been for sycamore trees, the tree sacred to Hathor and the goddess Anat. Many of the Hyksos kings are named after deities of the Canaanite pantheon. King 'Aper-'Anati is named after Anat, suggesting an affiliation with her. King Apophis had the same name as the serpent enemy of the sun god Ra. King Sakir-Har (1649 BC) is named after the Canaanite mountain god Harru, so this deity could also be added to the Hyksos pantheon.

Despite these distinctly foreign names, the kings Sakir-Har, Khayan and Apophis all adopted the Egyptian fivefold titulary, which suggests an acknowledgement of the Egyptian gods incorporated into these titles. However, it has been suggested that, rather than reflecting the Hyksos kings' religious beliefs, these names were produced by an Egyptian lector priest for propaganda purposes in order to give the impression that the Hyksos believed in the Egyptian pantheon. On a door jamb of Sakir-Har the inscription reads: '[Horus] the possessor of the Wadjet and Nekhbet diadems who subdues the bow people. The Golden Horus who establishes his boundary. The *hk3 h3swt*, Sakir-Har.' This could indicate a belief in the deities Horus, Wadjet and Nekhbet, although it is more likely that this text is reaffirming the legitimacy of Sakir-Har's rule by naming him as Horus under the protection of the double uraeus, consisting of the vulture and cobra goddesses.

A scribal palette of King Apophis uses the epithets 'the living image of Re', 'son of Wadjet', 'he whom Thoth instructed' and 'the scribe of Re' and shows an acknowledgement or even worship of the sun god Re. King Khayan Sewoseren*re*, Apophis Awoserre/Aqenen*re*/Nebkhepesh*re* and Khamudy Hotepibi*re* all incorporated the god Re in their prenomens. Also, the fact that Khayan usurped an earlier king's Ka statue from Bubastis and placed it in his Ka temple at Avaris suggests a belief in the Egyptian concept of the Ka and therefore in the afterlife.

Regardless of this evidence of the Hyksos religious affiliations, the Egyptian sources still claim that 'They ruled without Re' 'and did not serve any god which was in the entire land except Seth'. Despite the Egyptian propaganda texts, from the information available it would appear that the Hyksos had a pantheon of deities every bit as rich as the Egyptians', with a colourful combination of Egyptian and Canaanite deities.

Burials

There were eight types of tombs used in the Hyksos Period at Tell el Dab'a and all were Canaanite in design. Only one Egyptian-style limestone coffin has been found, and this contained a Canaanite burial of a contracted body accompanied by a Syro-Palestinian battleaxe and bronze dagger. It can be assumed that the Hyksos had a belief in the afterlife from a number of grave goods buried with them, including pottery, toggle pins, scarabs, weapons, beads and meat offerings.

The tomb orientation varied over time depending on the orientation of the buildings (houses or temples) in the close vicinity but as a rule the

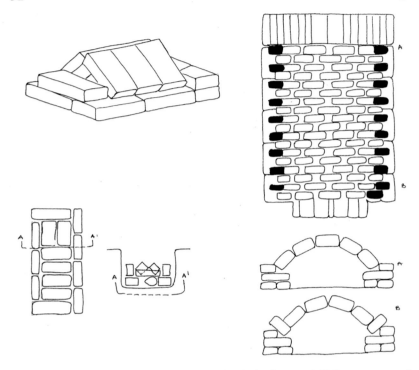

20. Three tomb designs of the Hyksos period. (Clockwise from top left) Superstructure of one tomb style – side view. Bird's-eye view of vaulted tomb with cross-sections of each end, marked A and B. Bird's-eye view of a brick tomb with cross-section (A) showing the position of the body under the roofing bricks. (Drawing by Charlotte Booth after Van den Brink, 1982)

head of the body faced the entrance of the tomb. The faces of the bodies were turned to either the east or the west, although a few examples faced upwards. There does not seem to be any significant connection between gender or age and the body's orientation. The bodies were buried in a contracted position – a practice that had not been carried out in Egypt since the Early Dynastic period for the poorer burials. It would appear that all through the Hyksos Period at Tell el Dab'a tombs and temples were built with a NNW–SSE orientation, which could have significance. The bodies facing the east or the west could reflect a belief in the sun god, and burials could therefore represent the death and rebirth of the sun as it did in the traditional Egyptian religion. The inconsistencies in orientation started occurring *c.*1660 BC, just before the Hyksos takeover, possibly at the time when there was an influx of

Canaanites into the area. These inconsistencies could therefore be attributed to space restrictions resulting from overcrowding rather than to a change in beliefs.

The most conspicuous Canaanite practice at Tell el Dab'a is that of the donkey burials. Seventeen donkey burials have been excavated at Avaris. It has been suggested that they were used to pull carts or the funerary carriage, although the only harness component found was one silver ring near the head of one of the donkeys. A few donkey burials have been found in Palestine at the sites of Tell el-Ajjul, Jericho and Lachish. However, these examples are earlier than the Hyksos Period and could suggest that this practice was brought to Egypt from Palestine. Horse burials in Cyprus from 800–700 BC show that pairs of horses were buried alive, or sacrificed by a blow to the head, still attached to the chariot that would have transported the deceased to the tomb. The donkeys at Tell el Dab'a may also have held a funerary function, although their practices are different from the Palestinian and the Cypriot examples. At Tell el Dab'a the donkeys are all buried complete, whereas in Palestine they all miss limbs – mostly the hindquarters – suggesting they were eaten as part of the funerary feast. Strangely enough, two donkeys were found buried in oval pits with no obvious connection to a tomb structure. They are sited in front of Temple V, although they are not contemporary with it.

Regardless of the purpose of the donkey burials, the practice indicates wealth and status, and in one instance five donkeys were buried in one pit, with one buried directly in front of the tomb entrance and two pairs buried behind it. This tomb would have belonged to a very wealthy member of Avaris society.

The other distinctive burial practice from Tell el Dab'a is that of servant burials. Servants are buried outside the tomb entrance with their faces turned towards it as if awaiting instruction from their dead master. One example has the servant buried some distance away from the tomb along with the five donkeys mentioned above and an ox, and there is little doubt that the servant and animals were buried at the same time as the tomb owner. The sacrifice of servants was practised in ancient Egypt but stopped at the end of the Predynastic period. If the Hyksos had ruled for longer they might have adopted the Egyptian practice of using shabti figures and tomb paintings to represent the objects and people required in the afterlife.

Communication between the Hyksos in Egypt and the Kerma Nubians appears to have been prevalent at this time, as the practice of servant burials suddenly appears in Nubia during this period. The Kerma servants would have suffocated by being buried alive inside the tomb. Since servant burials are not known in Syro-Palestine but are known in the

Levant, Canaan and Iraq (2600–2500 BC), this could be seen as an indicator of the origins of the Hyksos.

Another practice that reflects an ancient Egyptian ideology is the inclusion of ostrich eggshells in burials. It is thought that because some examples from Jericho are pierced at one end they might have contained a liquid offering. Whether the Tell el Dab'a examples were used for liquid offerings is uncertain, as all the examples are broken, although it seems likely. In the Predynastic period in Egypt ostriches were connected with a mother goddess cult – their inability to fly rendering them closer to the earth, as well as ostriches being very protective over their eggs. The eggs were included in many burials of the Predynastic period.

Food offerings were also left in the Tell el Dab'a tombs in order to nourish the deceased on their journey into whatever afterlife the Hyksos believed in. These offerings consisted of parts of oxen, sheep, goats, pigs, flamingos, geese, various ducks, and partridges. They were placed on plates or piled on the ground in the region of the burial pits. Pigs were often left as offerings at tombs but never in offering pits at the temple altars, except if they functioned as mortuary temples. Other food offerings were placed outside the tomb in chambers or in pits in the entrance. Sometimes the offering pits were reopened and fresh food was left for the enjoyment of the deceased.

The positioning of cemeteries in close proximity to the mortuary temples is an Egyptian religious custom, but having the mortuary complex close to the residential area is a Canaanite custom. It could indicate an ancestor cult, for whom the dead are a part of the life of the living. The burial of children under the age of two years was generally within the houses beneath the floor. They were placed in Palestinian amphora jars or replica vessels made of Nile mud. Each amphora would have contained a single child. There has been only one example of double burial, and this could suggest that the deceased were twins. The necks of the amphorae were broken to create a bigger opening and the body was placed within. The opening would then have been covered with a plate before burial.

Between 1660 and 1600 BC tombs were found very close to, or actually within, the houses in the form of pits sunken into the courtyards or beneath the floors. In periods of population overcrowding the community buried their dead under the houses in order to save space and to have their ancestors nearby, which supports the idea of an active ancestor cult. In 1600–1570 BC overcrowding had become a permanent problem and family chamber tombs were incorporated into the architecture of the new houses. There would be shafts dug down to numerous underground burial chambers with the entrance located in a special room or open courtyard that would have served as a chapel for making offerings. This tomb design would also have prevented the tombs from being robbed. For existing houses, there would have been a lean-to against an outer wall of the house that would have served as a chapel, or a secure room covering the burial shafts.

Ancestor worship appears to have been an important part of the religion, because of the close proximity of the burials to the houses. The niche near the entrance to Temple I has a libation plate sunk into the ground with pipes protruding from the ground, above a tomb from 1680–1660 BC. These pipes allowed liquid libations to be poured directly into the tomb from the outside. Oblations to this tomb had been practised for at least sixty years after the burial, indicating a prolonged ancestor cult. Similar installations in tombs have been found in coastal Syria.

In Temple I a deposit was made under an offering niche, indicating that offerings and libation ceremonies were a part of temple worship. This is both an Egyptian and a Canaanite practice, with the difference reflected by the excavation of pits in front of Temple III. These pits would have contained burnt offerings, which was a custom not commonly practised in Egypt.

Temple decoration from the Hyksos Period is scarce but we have evidence in Temple II and Temple III of azure-blue paint and on Temple II there are traces of painted figures, indicating that Hyksos temples would have been partially, if not fully, decorated. As both temples were painted the same colour, there could be some religious symbolism; blue symbolises water and sky and so an association with the storm god Ba'al is a possibility.

It is clear that the Hyksos were a very religious people, which is not surprising given that they had been born in Egypt and would have had the choice of either traditional Egyptian or traditional Canaanite practices. In the choice of deities there is a clear juxtaposition of the two cultures but in the burial practices the origins of the Hyksos are shown to be from the Syro-Palestinian area. Any culture settling into another country will adopt only a certain amount of the new culture, and it is normally the burial practices that are the last to change.

5
Contributions by the Hyksos to Egypt

The Hyksos are generally attributed with the introduction of the horse and chariot to Egypt, although the Egyptians learned the art of chariotry at the same time as the Hyksos in approximately 1600 BC, indicating that it may have been introduced by an independent source. Evidence shows that horses were present at Tell el Dab'a as horse teeth have been found here from the Hyksos Period (1610–1570 BC). Emery also discovered a horse burial at Buhen in Nubia, which was initially believed to be dated to the Middle Kingdom but may have dated to the Second Intermediate Period. The fact that horses were buried indicates that they were rare and valuable creatures. There is no evidence, either pictorial or archaeological, of a typical Hyksos chariot, but they probably resembled the early Eighteenth Dynasty models, which were lightweight with four-spoke wheels and a platform for two people, the driver and the archer. There would have been bow cases and quivers attached to the side of the chariot, leaving the riders' hands free. As chariots were light and could move large numbers of men quickly, they could open up the attack paths for the infantry behind. The architectural design of the

21. Stela of Amenhotep III practising archery from a chariot. (Luxor Museum. Photograph: Wayne Frostick)

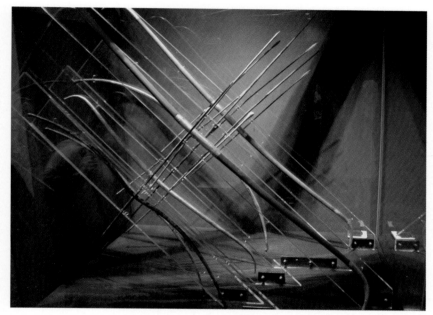

22. Composite and self-bows. (Luxor Museum. Photograph: Wayne Frostick)

Tell el-Yahudiyeh settlement and the Buhen fortress would have been an ideal defence against chariots as they would not have been able to advance over the sloping enclosure walls. If these structures were indeed contemporary with the Hyksos, it shows the builders were familiar with chariots and their limitations, so presumably they were also skilled in chariotry. The style of fort would also have been effective against the battering ram, which, although not generally thought to have been introduced into Egypt until the ninth century BC, is represented being used in the Middle Kingdom Beni Hasan tomb paintings by the Asiatics and therefore may have been familiar to the Hyksos.

In addition to learning the skills of the horse and chariot, the Hyksos introduced some Syro-Palestinian weaponry into Egypt. A number of Middle Kingdom tombs at Beni Hasan show Asiatics in battle using their traditional weapons, which include composite bows, spears, battleaxes and scimitars. Before the Hyksos Period the self-bow was used throughout Egypt; this was practically straight, with a slight bend at each end where the bowstring would have been attached. The composite bows introduced by the Hyksos were Old Akkadian in style, used in the Near East seven hundred years before reaching Egypt. This

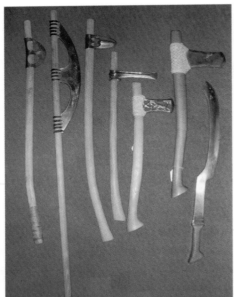

23. Reconstructions of Levantine weapons: (from left to right) Syrian epsilon or fenestrated socket axe, Middle Bronze Age I; Egyptian tanged crescentic axe, First Intermediate Period to Early Middle Kingdom; Syrian duckbill, Middle Bronze Age I/II – reconstructed bent-wood handle based on an example found at Baghouz; Syrian late Middle Bronze Age II socket chisel axe; Egyptian New Kingdom cut-out axe showing a lion attacking an ibex; Eighteenth Dynasty Egyptian battleaxe; late New Kingdom *khopesh*, a late evolution of the crescentic battleaxe adopted by Egypt from the Levant. (Photograph courtesy of Andrew Walpole)

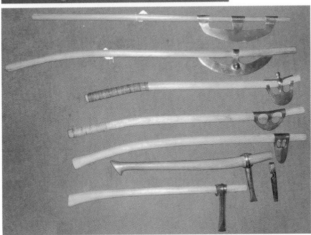

24. A chronological series of Levantine battleaxes, the earlier type generally being replaced by the next in line: (from top to bottom) Early Bronze Age III folded copper-sheet axe; single tanged cast copper crescentic axe based on an example from Tel el Hesi, Early Bronze Age III–II; 'anchor' axe, Early to Middle Bronze Age; fenestrated socket axe, Middle Bronze Age I; duckbill axe, Middle Bronze Age I–II; notched chisel axe, early Middle Bronze Age II; chisel axe, Middle Bronze Age II; chisel axe, late Middle Bronze Age II. (Photograph courtesy of Andrew Walpole)

bow had a dip in the centre where the archer would grip. It was made up of small fragments of wood stuck together rather than a single piece of wood, which gave it greater flexibility than the self-bow. Both bow types were used throughout the New Kingdom.

Various Syro-Palestinian daggers have been found at Tell el Dab'a in burials from the Hyksos Period. They were typical of the Middle Bronze Age II B style, which was used throughout the Near East during this period. The blades are attached to the handles by a small tang held on with rivets. Gradually they developed so that the tang extended to form the handle, and the handle was inlaid using wood or animal tooth. An example of this type of dagger was found in Saqqara in the tomb of the Semite Abed, inscribed with the cartouche of Apophis Akenenre. The inlay on the handle was missing but it would have been held in place by the edge of the handle being folded over it rather than by rivets. A similar dagger in the British Museum (BM 5425) has an inlaid handle of hippopotamus tooth or ivory but is not inscribed.

In the Beni Hasan tomb paintings the Asiatics are holding tang-type battleaxes, which originated in Mesopotamia but were also used in Palestine and Syria in the third millennium BC. They are first found in Egypt during the First Intermediate Period. There are two ways of connecting the blade to the handle: in 2850–2700 BC the middle tang would have been wrapped around the handle and in 2500–2100 BC the middle tang was attached to the handle by rivets. The blades were generally made of arsenical copper and bronze with acacia wood handles. The handles were sometimes wrapped in silver sheets, an example of which has been discovered in a warrior's tomb at Tell el Dab'a (1630–1610 BC).

The Hyksos are thought to have introduced the scimitar sword to Egypt as there is no evidence of this type of sword here before the Hyksos Period; however, the scimitar had been in use in Mesopotamia for over 750 years before reaching Egypt.

In addition to these bronze weapons, the Hyksos introduced a whole new military regime. The full-length body shield was introduced only in the Middle Kingdom, but the Egyptians quickly adopted the Hyksos' full body armour when trying to expel them from Egypt. After the Hyksos had been expelled, Egypt recognised her vulnerability and changed the way the army was organised. Although not a direct contribution of the Hyksos, it was their rise to the throne that encouraged the improvement of military skills in the New Kingdom.

Trade and political relations

As the Hyksos are considered to be Levantine in origin, it would be expected for there to have been a trade relationship between the Egyptian

Delta and the Levant, reflected in the material culture of Tell el Dab'a. A study was made of Canaanite amphorae found at Tell el Dab'a, using a technique called Neutron Activation Analysis (NAA), which can trace the country of origin of the clay used to make the pot. This study has shown that trade between the Delta and southern Palestine would have been essential to the economy of Tell el Dab'a. Seventy-four per cent of the pottery tested was made from foreign clay and appears to have been imported from southern Palestine. There were, however, no pottery examples from Syria or northern Palestine.

It is thought that a large number of goods would have been imported from southern Palestine, including copper, tin, battleaxes, daggers, bronze belts, jewellery and silver. From northern Syria cylinder seals, wood and metal may have been imported, all of which would not have been stored or transported in pottery vessels and therefore may not be present in the archaeological record. Based on the number of Canaanite amphorae already found, it is suggested that there may be as many as two million of these jars at Tell el Dab'a. This indicates that over the 250 years of the history of Tell el Dab'a eight thousand jars a year would be imported, making a rate of twenty jars a day.

This vast number of imports would have been possible only by sea, and excavations at Tell el Dab'a have uncovered a major harbour site, which would have housed numerous trade ships. The shipping season was between May and October, and over three hundred ships could be in harbour in this period. The Kamose stela mentions the ships docked in the harbour of Avaris, piled high with imported goods, which Kamose promptly commandeered: 'ships of new cedar, filled with gold, lapis lazuli, silver, turquoise and innumerable bronze battleaxes, apart from *moringa* oil, incense, fat, honey, *itrn* wood, *ssndm* wood, *spny* wood … all the good products of Retjenu'.

In addition to this large number of imported pottery vessels there are also many Canaanite-style vessels made from local materials, indicating that the settled population was of foreign origin. The Canaanite amphora jars would have held up to 30 litres and were considered the best vessels for the import of liquids. This type of jar would have been used for the storage and transportation of food and liquids until the Ptolemaic period (third century BC). Residue left at the bottom of two amphorae shows traces of tartaric acid, one of the components of grape wine, and indicates that wine would have been one of the imports. There is evidence of wine production at Tell el Dab'a, showing that not all wine would have been imported. A plaster-lined basin with draining channels from the early New Kingdom has been excavated, although there were no traces of tartaric acid within the basin. Evidence from the excavations indicates that olive oil, tree resins, incense and honey were also imported in

25. Tell el-Yahudiyeh ware – white-painted juglet. (Copyright: Petrie Museum of Egyptian Archaeology, University College London, UC 13453)

amphorae, and it would appear that the jars themselves were used for storage as well as for transportation. Items imported to Avaris would have been distributed throughout Lower and Middle Egypt, the areas governed by the Hyksos. The Delta would also have controlled the trade of Egyptian goods (food, wine, papyrus). Thebes would therefore have had an economic reason to start a war of retaliation north of Cusae against the Hyksos.

The most common pottery style from the Hyksos Period is Tell el-Yahudiyeh ware, imported into Egypt in the Thirteenth Dynasty from northern Palestine and Byblos and gradually spreading throughout Egypt as far south as Kush. It was primarily used as a funerary item. Tell el-Yahudiyeh ware consists mostly of juglets with dark

26. Tell el-Yahudiyeh ware – white-painted juglet. (Copyright: Petrie Museum of Egyptian Archaeology, University College London, UC 13454)

27. Tell el-Yahudiyeh ware – vertical bands of herringbone design. (Copyright: Petrie Museum of Egyptian Archaeology, University College London, UC 13460)

brown-black or red polished surfaces decorated with white paste in comb-pricked impressions. The widest variety throughout Egypt has been found at Tell el Dab'a. Different decorative markings could indicate what oils or substances were stored or imported within the containers. The residues of the contents are not easily identified, but we know they consist of vegetable and animal fats. The juglets have very narrow necks, allowing only a small amount of liquid to be poured at a time.

Tell el-Yahudiyeh ware has also been discovered in Cyprus made of Egyptian materials and in Egypt made of Cypriot materials. This implies that between 1750 and 1680 BC either there was a Cypriot community living at Tell el Dab'a or, more likely, there was a trade relationship between Egypt and Cyprus. In 1750 BC, before the Hyksos takeover, the pottery examples found at Tell el Dab'a were primarily Syro-Palestinian in

28. Tell el-Yahudiyeh ware – diagonal punctured-lines design. (Copyright: Petrie Museum of Egyptian Archaeology, University College London, UC 13465)

origin, revealing a multicultural society in this city. This was when the first major influx of settlers from the Levant arrived in Egypt, probably drafted into the army or employed as shipbuilders or craftsmen.

Apart from the Tell el-Yahudiyeh ware travelling to Kush, the only recorded link between Kush and the Hyksos is from the letter of King Apophis recorded in the Kamose stela. Apophis asks the Kushite kings

29. The Sphinx of Khayan from Baghdad. (Photograph courtesy of The Trustees of The British Museum, EA 987)

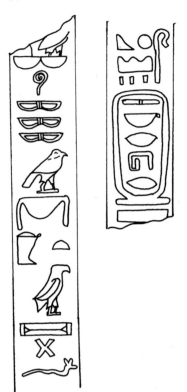

30. Door jamb of Sakir-Har. (Drawing by Charlotte Booth after Bietak, 1996)

for help against the Theban Seventeenth Dynasty. If the Kushites had joined with the Hyksos the alliance would have been a major threat to Thebes, as both the Hyksos and the Kushites could have raised large armies to attack Thebes from the north and south. To change this situation, the Theban dynasties instigated the battles leading to the expulsion of the Hyksos as a way of taking control of the situation by gaining mastery of Lower Egypt. Very little Lower Egyptian pottery has been discovered in Nubia and very little Nubian pottery has been discovered in Lower Egypt, suggesting that the relationship between the Hyksos and the Kushites was not very strong. The content of King Apophis' letter hints at this unstable relationship. Apophis asks the Kushite king, 'Why have you risen as ruler without letting me know?' If trade relations had been closer Apophis would have known who the king of Kush was. The Hyksos ruler was probably trying to start an alliance with Kush, although the Kushite ruler would no doubt have

31. The Sphinx of Apophis. (The British Museum. Photograph: Wayne Frostick)

been wary of antagonising the Theban rulers, who were nearer to Kush than the Hyksos.

The discovery of elite Egyptian objects abroad indicates that foreign alliances were sealed with diplomatic gifts. These objects include an alabaster vase lid inscribed with King Khayan's cartouche found at Knossos in Crete. Before the Hyksos Period contact had been made with Crete, and in the New Kingdom Minoan frescoes at Tell el Dab'a suggest a continued relationship. An obsidian vase fragment also inscribed with the cartouche of Khayan was discovered in Hattusha (modern Bogazköy in Turkey), the Hittite capital. The Hyksos could have been attempting to make alliances with Egypt's enemies to aid them in the inevitable attack that the Theban Dynasties would stage upon Avaris. A sphinx, again commissioned by Khayan, was discovered in Baghdad. Despite these diplomatic gifts from the Hyksos ruler, no parallel gifts from the foreign rulers have been found in Egypt.

However, for all these efforts at political relations with the enemies of Egypt, the door jamb of Sakir-Har from Tell el Dab'a uses purely Egyptian prejudices when referring to the traditional enemies of Egypt: 'The possessor of the Wadjet and Nekhbet diadems, who subdues the bow people'. The description 'bow people' is a reference to the traditional nine enemies of Egypt, of which the Asiatics are one and the Nubians are another. It would seem that the Hyksos were ruling Egypt as Egyptians and may have been trying to unite the traditional enemies of Egypt for one of two reasons: either to make Egypt a stronger political force against the rest of the world, or to secure aid for themselves should the Theban armies retaliate against Hyksos rule. Either way, Egypt would have been a more politically stable country with such a support network.

The movement of Egyptian monuments also hints at relationships with foreign lands current at the time. During the reign of Apophis, sculptures looted from Egyptian temples and cemeteries were transported to Canaan and Syria. This does indicate that even if the Hyksos did not originate in this area there was trade between the regions.

Four royal seals were discovered in Geser, Tell Zafit and Jericho dated to the Hyksos Fifteenth Dynasty. These seals represent the presence of Hyksos officials in the area, suggesting these regions were allies or possibly vassals of the Hyksos kingdom. Political alliances may have been formed through diplomatic marriages and there is some evidence for this. In the Theban tomb of Amenhotep I a vase fragment was discovered with the names of Apophis Awoserre and his daughter Harath. Because the tomb is in Thebes it has been suggested that Apophis' daughter was the child of a diplomatic marriage between the Fifteenth and Seventeenth Dynasties. Another possible Theban marriage with the Hyksos dynasty is that of the Princess Tany and Apophis. Their names appear together on an offering stand usurped from the Twelfth Dynasty and on a stela, both found at Tell el Dab'a. Princess Tany is thought to be a princess of the Seventeenth Dynasty as her name is of Theban origin. It has been suggested that she may have held property in the Delta or, more dramatically, could even have been a hostage of the Hyksos. Even if these diplomatic marriages did not take place, it seems that there was not much Theban resentment of the Hyksos rulers until the later Seventeenth Dynasty kings.

In addition to the import of weapons and pottery, the later Hyksos kings were interested in literature and copies of some of the most important earlier papyri were produced during this period. The Middle Kingdom collection of stories known as *Papyrus Westcar* is dated to the Hyksos Period and is the only surviving copy of the tale of the birth of the Fifth Dynasty kings. Another text was the *Rhind Mathematical Papyrus*, dated to the thirty-third year of King Apophis' reign.

6
Expulsion of the Hyksos

The Theban Seventeenth Dynasty, in the reign of King Seqenenre Tao II, started a campaign to expel the Hyksos kings from Egypt. This campaign was continued and completed by Seqenenre Tao's sons Kamose and Ahmose I, the latter being the first king of the Eighteenth Dynasty. The hostilities between the Theban Dynasty and the Hyksos are first recorded in the *Sallier I Papyrus*, which tells a story of the Hyksos king Apophis approaching Seqenenre Tao complaining that his hippopotamus pool in Thebes was keeping him awake in the Delta. Although the distance between Thebes and the Delta makes this unlikely

to be true, the complaint sparks off the hostilities between the two rulers. Seqenenre Tao embarked on his campaign to push the Hyksos out of the Theban area, resulting in his death. His mummy shows that he died on the battlefield from numerous wounds to the head. His campaign was continued by Kamose, who recorded the battle on the Kamose stela. This would originally have been set up at Karnak temple, as one of a pair. The text from one of the stelae continued on to the other rather than the second being a copy of the first, which in itself was unusual. The campaign is also recorded on the Carnarvon Tablet number 1, which belongs to a pair of hieratic writing boards found on a ledge near the entrance to a plundered

32. Kamose stela. (Luxor Museum. Photograph: Wayne Frostick)

tomb near Deir el-Bahri. It is thought that this tablet was created at the time of the battle, or not more than fifty years later, and it may have been a copy of the Kamose stela.

The tablet explains the political situation of the time from the view point of Kamose: 'one prince in Avaris and another is in Kush ... each holding his slice of the black land [Egypt] – who share this land with me.' This clearly indicates that even during the reign of Kamose, despite the struggles of his father, Egypt was a divided land, with the north and the south each having a different ruler. The threat from the Hyksos and the Kushites would have put the Theban dynasty in a vulnerable position, as it could be attacked from both the north and the south simultaneously. Kamose therefore expresses his desire in the Carnarvon Tablet to unite Egypt: 'I will grapple with him [Apophis] that I may cleave open his belly – my desire is to deliver Egypt and to smite the A'amu [Asiatics].'

The campaign of the Theban Dynasties was one of destruction, with everything in their path being laid to waste. The Carnarvon Tablet records that all the 'spelt is sent to our swine', indicating that they fed the wheat to the pigs as a means of destroying what belonged to the Hyksos.

When Kamose's forces reached Middle Egypt, Apophis and his army retreated northwards towards the eastern Delta. Kamose stood outside the reinforced walls of Avaris taunting Apophis, who was barricaded inside. Apophis refused to fight, so Kamose returned to Thebes claiming a triumph. Although Kamose did not capture Avaris his campaign was considered a success as he led his forces over the Hyksos border at Cusae, overcame provinces governed by Egyptian vassals of the Hyksos at Hermopolis and marched his way into the Delta. Kamose also sent troops to the Bahriya Oasis to prevent the Nubians and Hyksos from communicating. He had probably also taken control of Lower Nubia to reinforce the Egyptian power in this area.

After the death of Kamose, his brother Ahmose continued with the campaign against the Hyksos. The Hyksos were now ruled by Khamudy, following the death of Apophis. In Ahmose's campaign he first took Sile on the Egypt–Sinai border, cutting contact between the Hyksos and Canaan as a precaution against reinforcements arriving from this region. Then he besieged and captured Avaris. In the tomb of Ahmose, son of Ebana, at El Kab there is a description of how the king drove the Hyksos out of Avaris and chased them until they reach Sharuhen in Palestine. There is also evidence that all of the towns on the way to this city were sacked by the Egyptians. After a three-year siege at Sharuhen, Ahmose finally defeated the Hyksos and returned to Egypt. Ahmose recorded his victory over the Hyksos at his temple at Abydos, but unfortunately the remains are very badly damaged.

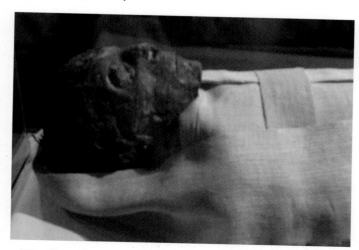

33. Mummy of Ahmose. (Luxor Museum. Photograph: Geoff Webb)

The Egyptian reports of the Hyksos being barbarians appear to be unfounded. If the Hyksos had not taken the opportunity to grasp the throne when it was available another foreign group might have done so – and one, perhaps, whose main ambition was to take the wealth of Egypt and pass it to their country of origin.

The downfall of the Hyksos was probably a result of the personal ambition and greed of Apophis. If he had continued ruling the country in the same way as Khayan had done previously, by striving to form alliances with enemies and by building temples and dedicating statues to the Egyptian religion, the reign of the Hyksos could well have lasted another hundred years. However, as the *Sallier I Papyrus* tells us, he antagonised the Theban king, looted temples and sent usurped statues abroad. It would seem that although the Hyksos did not leave any huge monumental buildings and statues, they did contribute enormously to the wealth of Egypt. Whether this was motivated by their fear of being ruled by foreigners again is not clear, but there can be no doubt that Egypt became a stronger nation because of them.

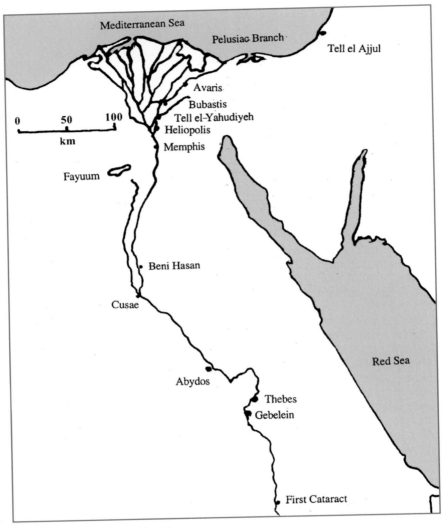

34. Map of Egypt and the Near East.

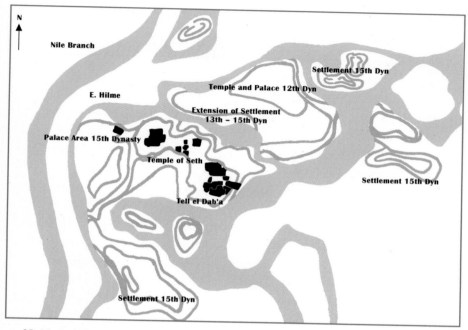

35. Map of Tell el Dab'a showing the mounds upon which the settlement was situated. (Adapted from Bietak, 1996; drawing by Charlotte Booth)

7
Further reading

Bietak, M. *Avaris and Pi-Ramesse: Archaeological Exploration in the Eastern Nile Delta.* Oxford University Press, 1979.

Bietak, M. *The Capital of the Hyksos: Recent Excavations at Tell el Dab'a.* British Museum Press, 1996.

Breasted, J. H. *Ancient Records of Egypt,* volume 2, 303, 125. University of Chicago Press, 1906.

Dawson, W. R. 'A bronze dagger of the Hyksos Period', *Journal of Egyptian Archaeology,* 11 (1925), 216–17.

Gardiner, A. *The Admonitions of an Egyptian Sage: From a Hieratic Papyrus in Leiden.* J. C. Hinrichs' Sche Buchhandlung, Leipzig, 1906.

Habachi, L. *The 2nd Stela of Kamose and His Struggle against the Hyksos Ruler and His Capital.* Abhandlungen der Deutschen Archaologischen Instituts Kairo Agyptische Reiche, Glukstadt, 1972.

Harvey, S. 'Monuments of Ahmose at Abydos', *Egyptian Archaeology,* 4 (1999), 3–5.

Heinsohn, G. 'Who were the Hyksos? Can archaeology and stratigraphy provide a solution to the "enigma of world history"?', *Atti del VI Congresso Internazionale di Eggittologia,* 2 (1993), 207–19. Comitato Organizzativo del Congresso, Turin.

Newberry, P. E. *Beni Hassan,* volumes 1 and 2. Archaeological Survey of Egypt, Egypt Exploration Fund, 1893–4.

Oren, E. D. (editor). *The Hyksos: New Historical and Archaeological Perspectives.* University of Philadelphia Press, 1997. All of the articles in this book are very useful.

Petrie, W. M. F. *Hyksos and Israelite Cities.* Bernard Quartich, London, 1906.

Redford, D. M. *Egypt, Canaan and Israel in Ancient Times.* Princeton University Press, New Jersey, 1992.

Ryholt, R. S. B. *The Political Situation in Egypt During the Second Intermediate Period.* Museum Tusculanum Press, Copenhagen, 1997.

Save-Soderbergh, T. 'The Hyksos rule in Egypt', *Journal of Egyptian Archaeology*, 37 (1937), 54–71.

Van den Brink, E. C. M. *Tombs and Burial Customs at Tell el Dab'a*. Universitat Wien, Austria, 1982.

Yadin, Y. 'Hyksos fortifications and the battering ram', *Bulletin of the American Schools of Oriental Research*, 137 (1955), 29–31.

8
Museums to visit

United Kingdom
The British Museum, Great Russell Street, London WC1B 3DG.
Telephone: 020 7323 8000. Website: www.thebritishmuseum.ac.uk
Fitzwilliam Museum, Trumpington Street, Cambridge CB2 1RB.
Telephone: 01223 332900. Website: www.fitzmuseum.cam.ac.uk
National Museum of Scotland, Chambers Street, Edinburgh EH1 1JF.
Telephone: 0131 247 4422. Website: www.nms.ac.uk
Petrie Museum of Egyptian Archaeology, University College London,
Malet Place, London WC1E 6BT. Telephone: 020 7679 2884. Website:
www.petrie.ucl.ac.uk

Austria
The Vienna Kunsthistorisches Museum, Main Building, Maria Theresien-
Platz, 1010 Vienna. Telephone: (+431) 525 24 403. Website:
www.khm.at

Egypt
Egyptian Museum, Tahrir Square, Kasr el-Nil, Cairo. Telephone: (+20)
2 575 4267. Website: www.egyptianmuseum.gov.eg
Luxor Museum of Ancient Egyptian Art, Luxor.

United States
Metropolitan Museum of Art, 1000 5th Avenue at 82nd Street, New
York, NY 10028 0198. Telephone: (+1) 212 535 7710. Website:
www.metmuseum.org

Index

(Page numbers in italics refer to illustrations)